URSA

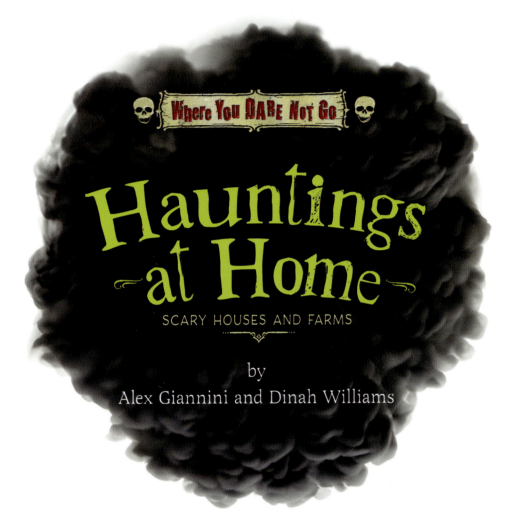

Where You DARE Not Go

Hauntings at Home

SCARY HOUSES AND FARMS

by
Alex Giannini and Dinah Williams

BEARPORT
PUBLISHING

Minneapolis, Minnesota

Credits

Cover and title page, © Lovely Bird/Shutterstock, © Independent birds/Shutterstock, © Eddie J. Rodriquez/Shutterstock, and © F Armstrong Photography/Shutterstock; 4–5, © Jeanne McRight/Shutterstock, © Marcin Perkowski/Shutterstock, and © Tkjmbatt/iStock; 6, © Hemis/Alamy and © Hemis/Alamy; 8, © Lee Boxleitner/Shutterstock; 9, © Taber Photographic Co./Wikimedia Commons; 10, © The Reading Room/Alamy; 11, © David L. Trafton/Wikimedia Commons and © Benjamin Clapp/Shutterstock; 12, © LongLiveRock/Creative Commons Attribution 2.0 Generic; 13, © Burns Archive/Wikimedia Commons, © Burns Archive/Wikimedia Commons, and © Public Domain/Wikimedia Commons; 14, © Public Domain; 15, © Kiselev Andrey Valerevich/Shutterstock; 16, © Robert Thivierge/Creative Commons Attribution-Share Alike 3.0 Unported; 17, © Max Sky/Shutterstock; 18, © Doug Kerr/Creative Commons Attribution-Share Alike 2.0 Generic; 19, © Eric Isselee/Shutterstock, © Zayats Svetlana/Shutterstock, © Nataliia K/Shutterstock, and © Nataliia K/Shutterstock; 20, © Historic American Buildings Survey/Wikimedia Commons and © Historic American Buildings Survey/Wikimedia Commons; 21, © Melinda Nagy/Shutterstock; 22, © THEPALMER/iStock, © Andrea Izzotti/Shutterstock, and © Mathew Brady/Wikimedia Commons PD-US; 23, © Mathew Brady/Wikimedia Commons PD-US and © Public Domain/Wikimedia Commons; 24, © Marathon/Creative Commons Attribution-Share Alike 2.0 Generic; 25, © NeoStocks/Shutterstock; 26, © Brian Stansberry/Creative Commons Attribution 4.0 International; 27, © Public Domain/Wikimedia Commons PD-US and © New Africa/Shutterstock; 28, © wanderluster/iStock; 29, © wanderluster/iStock; 30, © Jim Evans/Creative Commons Attribution-Share Alike 3.0 Unported; 31, © Donna Beeler/Shutterstock; 32, © Public Domain; 33, © josefauer/Shutterstock; 34, © Historic American Buildings Survey/Wikimedia Commons and © Carol M. Highsmith Archive/Wikimedia Commons; 35, © Mathew Benjamin Brady/Wikimedia Commons and © JCDH/Shutterstock; 36, © Jason McLaren/Creative Commons Attribution-Share Alike 4.0 International and © The Day Book/Wikimedia Commons; 37, © Maksim Nikalayenka/Shutterstock; 38, © Debbie Ann Powell/Shutterstock; 39, © Urban Walnut/Creative Commons Attribution-Share Alike 3.0 Unported; 40, © Connecticut State Library/WPA Architectural Survey; 41, © LiliGraphie/Shutterstock, © Yogi Kichiro/Shutterstock, and © RonnyKratif/Shutterstock.

Bearport Publishing Company Product Development Team

President: Jen Jenson; Director of Product Development: Spencer Brinker; Managing Editor: Allison Juda; Associate Editor: Naomi Reich; Associate Editor: Tiana Tran; Art Director: Colin O'Dea; Designer: Kim Jones; Designer: Kayla Eggert; Product Development Assistant: Owen Hamlin

Statement on Usage of Generative Artificial Intelligence

Bearport Publishing remains committed to publishing high-quality nonfiction books. Therefore, we restrict the use of generative AI to ensure accuracy of all text and visual components pertaining to a book's subject. See BearportPublishing.com for details.

Library of Congress Cataloging-in-Publication Data

Names: Giannini, Alex, author. | Williams, Dinah (Dinah J.) author.
Title: Hauntings at home : scary houses and farms / by Alex Giannini and Dinah Williams.
Description: Minneapolis, Minnesota : Bearport Publishing, [2025] | Series: Where you dare not go | Includes bibliographical references and index.
Identifiers: LCCN 2024004272 (print) | LCCN 2024004273 (ebook) | ISBN 9798892320733 (hardcover) | ISBN 9798892326056 (paperback) | ISBN 9798892322065 (ebook)
Subjects: LCSH: Haunted houses--Juvenile literature. | Ghosts--Juvenile literature.
Classification: LCC BF1475 .G53 2025 (print) | LCC BF1475 (ebook) | DDC 133.1/22--dc23/eng/20240228
LC record available at https://lccn.loc.gov/2024004272
LC ebook record available at https://lccn.loc.gov/2024004273

Copyright © 2025 Bearport Publishing Company. All rights reserved. No part of this publication may be reproduced in whole or in part, stored in any retrieval system, or transmitted in any form or by any means, electronic, mechanical, photocopying, recording, or otherwise, without written permission from the publisher. Bearport Publishing is a division of Chrysalis Education Group.

For more information, write to Bearport Publishing, 5357 Penn Avenue South, Minneapolis, MN 55419.

Contents

Home Scary Home! 4
Thieves in the Night 6
Building a Home for Ghosts 8
Kinderhook's Ghosts 10
The Bloody End to the Bordens 12
The Harrisville Haunting 14
Death at the Deane 16
The House of Horror 18
The Dying Room 20
Lincoln Can't Leave 22
"I Will Do It" 24
The Bell Witch 26
The Problem with Poison 28
A Glamorous Ghost 30
A Ghostly Murder 32
The Coffin in the Cellar 34
The 2:00 a.m. Train 36
The White Witch 38
A Bloody Battle 40

A World of . . . Hauntings at Home 42
Glossary 44
Read More 46
Learn More Online 46
Index 47

Home Scary Home!

There is something frightening about a creaky, old house or a deserted, lonely farm. What might have happened there? You've heard stories about crimes, deaths, and mysterious disappearances. But those were just stories, right?

Suddenly, you hear a strange *thud... thud... thud...* coming from inside the building. You turn your head as a crow swoops down from a dead tree. In the window, you're sure you see a floating, glowing shape, and then you hear a scream!

Thieves in the Night

CHRETIEN POINT PLANTATION
SUNSET, LOUISIANA

The 3,000-acre (1,200-ha) Chretien Point Plantation in Sunset, Louisiana, has a thrilling history. Tales of bandits only add to its lore. Do terrifying thieves still haunt the property in search of treasure? Decide for yourself. . . .

Chretien Point Plantation

Felicité Chretien

Hippolyte Chretien completed construction of his two-story mansion in 1835. He was a successful businessman who buried his fortune on his property. When he died of yellow fever just four years later, his wife, Felicité, was left in charge of the farm and the money. Unfortunately, news about her wealth attracted thieves.

Late one night as Felicité slept, a group of bandits quietly crept across the front lawn. They hid behind giant oak trees on the property. Felicité heard a noise and sprang out of bed. She looked out her window and saw the men heading for the house. Meanwhile, one of them had made his way inside. She called for help, but it was too late—Felicité found herself face-to-face with one of the bandits. Luckily, she was armed. She pulled out a small gun and shot the thief dead. When the other thieves heard the gun, they fled.

Today, a stain of the dead bandit's blood remains on the stairs where he died. Visitors to the plantation have heard Felicité's voice call out in the darkness. They say her spirit wanders the house, reliving that night. Many have also seen the thief she killed, still walking the property in search of Felicité's fortune.

Battles were fought on the plantation's grounds during the U.S. Civil War (1861–1865). There's a bullet hole in the front door from the war.

Building a Home for Ghosts

MYSTERIOUS WINCHESTER HOUSE
SAN JOSE, CALIFORNIA

Few things are scarier than being chased by an angry ghost. Unless, of course, it is being chased by a huge crowd of ghosts. Sarah Winchester would know. She spent almost half her life trying to outrun thousands of angry spirits.

Sarah Winchester's House

Sarah Winchester believed in ghosts. After her husband, William, died in 1881, she was sad and wanted to talk to him one last time. So, Sarah hired a medium to contact his spirit. What she learned would forever change her life.

Through the medium, William told Sarah that the millions of dollars he had left her were cursed. The money had been earned by selling deadly Winchester rifles. Sarah had to build a house for the spirits of the thousands of people killed by the guns. As long as she kept building, the ghosts would not kill her.

What could Sarah do? She bought a six-room house in 1884 and began building. Thirty-eight years later, the maze-like house had 160 rooms. Even though workmen built around the clock, death finally found Sarah. She died at age 83 in 1922. Today, visitors to the house can find Sarah, too—her ghost has been seen wandering its many hallways!

Sarah Winchester

Sarah found comfort in the number 13, which she considered lucky. In her house, there are 13 bathrooms, 13 windows in some rooms, 13 palm trees lining the main driveway, and 13 stairs on most of the staircases.

Kinderhook's Ghosts

JESSE MERWIN FARMHOUSE
KINDERHOOK, NEW YORK

Hauntings are common in Kinderhook, a small town in New York that dates back to the 1650s. "This area has always been loaded with ghost stories," says a local historian. Could that have something to do with a famous spooky legend?

Jesse Merwin Farmhouse

In 1820, author Washington Irving, who lived in Kinderhook for several years, wrote a popular ghost story called *The Legend of Sleepy Hollow*. In his story, a schoolteacher named Ichabod Crane comes face-to-face with a horrifying headless horseman. Irving based the Ichabod Crane character on his close friend, schoolteacher Jesse Merwin.

Jesse Merwin lived in a large farmhouse in Kinderhook, which Irving often visited. Years later, in 1941, Ben and Esther Tuttle bought Merwin's farmhouse. Members of the Tuttle family experienced weird happenings there. The children saw an apparition flickering on the porch. Visitors witnessed bedroom doors swinging open in the middle of the night.

Jesse Merwin

Long ago, Merwin's gravestone was placed facedown to create the front step of the house. It's said that if the stone is moved, the headless horseman will appear and ride again. Esther Tuttle tried moving the stone once, and that same night, lightning struck the house. She never touched it again.

Esther didn't let the ghosts scare her at first. "We figured if we had ghosts, they were the friendly sort," she said.

The Bloody End to the Bordens

LIZZIE BORDEN HOUSE
FALL RIVER, MASSACHUSETTS

People who die in violent and unexpected ways are thought to be more likely to return as ghosts. Perhaps they are seeking revenge for their murders. Or maybe they don't know they are dead. Few died as suddenly and violently as Abby and Andrew Borden, so it's no wonder they are still at home.

Lizzie Borden House

On the hot morning of August 4, 1892, Abby Borden was making a bed in the guest room of her home. Someone came up behind her and crushed her head with 19 blows from an axe. About 90 minutes later, her husband, Andrew, was killed in the same way. Some people thought that their daughter, Lizzie, committed the crime. However, there was not enough evidence to prove it.

Lizzie Borden

Today, the Borden house is an inn where people can spend the night. Yet guests should beware. Some visitors say they have heard the voice of a woman quietly crying. Others have reported seeing an older woman dressed in clothes from the 1890s cleaning the guest room. They have even been awakened in the middle of the night to see this same woman tucking them into bed. Maybe it is the ghost of Abby, still making the same bed all these years later.

Lizzie's parents after the murder

Using photos from the Borden crime scene, the owners of the inn have re-created the way the rooms looked on the day that Lizzie's parents were killed. They also serve a breakfast similar to the one that the Bordens ate the morning they died.

The Harrisville Haunting

THE OLD ARNOLD ESTATE
HARRISVILLE, RHODE ISLAND

The terror began at 5:15 each morning at the Old Arnold Estate. It started when the smell of rotting flesh floated through the house. The Perron family knew that the stench could mean only one thing—the ghosts were back!

The Old Arnold Estate

In 1971, Roger and Carolyn Perron, along with their five daughters, moved into the Old Arnold Estate, a historic farmhouse in Rhode Island. Soon after, unexplained horrors overtook the house.

Unseen spirits that stank of rotting flesh would fly into the bedrooms. The ghosts tossed beds in the air and dragged the children across the floor. On several occasions, the cruel attacks left bruises and drew blood.

The Arnold Estate's most frightening ghost was named Bathsheba Sherman, who was a former resident of the home. During her lifetime, townspeople believed Bathsheba was a witch who had killed a baby as an offering to the devil. One night, Carolyn Perron awoke to find an old woman hovering over her bed. The spectral figure screamed, "Get out! Get out! I'll drive you out with death and gloom!" Finally, in 1980, the Perrons—fearful for their lives—moved out of their haunted farmhouse. They never looked back.

Later, the Perrons learned that their home was the site of several ghastly deaths. Could that explain why so many restless souls haunt the house?

Death at the Deane

THE DEANE HOUSE
CALGARY, ALBERTA, CANADA

A boardinghouse is a building where people rent rooms for short periods of time. With so many guests, a boardinghouse is bound to have a rich history. The Deane House is no exception. C. L. Jacques began renting rooms to people there in 1929. According to some, a few of his guests have never left.

The Deane House

One of the many staff members who saw the Deane House ghosts was Alez Jackci. He was working late one night when a man floated down the hallway. The bottoms of his legs were missing. The ghost went down the stairs and out the door. Others have heard loud footsteps on the top floor. According to legend, there is a bloodstain in the attic that will not go away—no matter how much it is cleaned.

Why are there so many ghosts at the Deane House? When it was a boardinghouse, a number of unusual deaths took place there. One young woman jumped from the second-story window. A man was shot on the porch. In 1952, a husband stabbed his wife to death. He then killed himself. Perhaps the spirits of these victims are not ready to leave yet. One thing is certain, however. With so many ghosts, the Deane House is one of Canada's most haunted places.

The ghost of a First Nations man has often been spotted at the Deane House. Some say this is because the house was built on an old burial ground. One woman who went into the basement was greeted by the spirit. He told her that the site was sacred and she shouldn't be there. He then disappeared.

The House of Horror

AMITYVILLE HOUSE, AMITYVILLE, NEW YORK

A poltergeist is a spirit that makes itself known in a home by making loud noises and moving objects. In some cases, it can also hurt people. Poltergeists, however, seem calm compared with the angry spirits that may have terrorized a house in Amityville, New York.

The house in Amityville

On the night of November 14, 1974, 23-year-old Ronald DeFeo, Jr., took out his rifle and shot his father. Within the next 15 minutes, he would murder all 6 members of his family. The brutal crime made headlines in many newspapers. Unfortunately, this was not the last time people would hear about shocking events taking place in this house.

One year later, the Lutz family moved in. In the 28 days they lived there, they claimed the house began to change. Flies started swarming around the windows. Slime oozed from the walls. Toilet bowls began to turn black.

The Lutzes' daughter developed a disturbing imaginary friend. It was a pig named Jodie, and it seemed very real. Her parents saw its glowing red eyes, heard its squeal, and even saw the animal's hoofprints in the snow. Other creepy events also took place in the house. Mrs. Lutz claimed invisible hands grabbed her. Unable to stand the haunting any longer, the family fled one night, never to return.

Many people who have investigated the Amityville haunting believe most of the terrifying events described by the Lutzes never happened. But that hasn't stopped thousands of people from being fascinated by the house's famous and spooky past.

The Dying Room

MAGNOLIA PLANTATION, DERRY, LOUISIANA

There are many legends of ghosts that haunt the grounds of Louisiana's mansions. At Magnolia Plantation, in Derry, the property's disturbing history could help explain the ghostly goings-on.

Magnolia Plantation

The overseer's house

In the mid-1800s at Magnolia Plantation, enslaved workers decided to fight back against their cruel treatment. Legend has it that a group of workers captured one of the cruelest overseers. They took him to a secret place called the Dying Room, where it's believed they killed him. It's said that his face can still be seen in an upstairs window—eyes wide with terror and mouth twisted in pain.

More than 100 years later, a young descendent of one of Magnolia's original owners experienced a ghostly visit. He was playing alone on the second floor of the house. When his parents entered the room to check on him, an unseen force slapped each of them on the back of the neck. Were spirits from the past returning to haunt them?

In 2005, Kenneth Brown, an anthropologist from Texas, visited the plantation to look for artifacts. He found an old gold charm that showed a figure standing on a pile of snakes. Kenneth also reported objects that mysteriously moved on their own and an odd yellow powder spread across a doorway. It seems there's much left to uncover at this creepy farm.

The main house on the Magnolia property was badly damaged during the Civil War. In 1897, its owners rebuilt the house to look exactly like the original.

Lincoln Can't Leave

THE WHITE HOUSE, WASHINGTON, D.C.

Many ghosts are said to haunt the White House. The ghost of President Andrew Jackson has been spotted there, as well as Dolley Madison, the wife of President James Madison. The most famous ghostly visitor, however, is Abraham Lincoln.

The White House

President Abraham Lincoln

Mary Todd Lincoln

One morning in the spring of 1865, Abraham Lincoln woke from a terrible dream. In it, he saw guards stationed around a corpse in the White House. When he asked who was dead, a soldier replied, "The President was killed by an assassin." Less than a month later, on April 14, 1865, Lincoln was shot to death by John Wilkes Booth.

Since his death, Lincoln's ghost has been seen a number of times at the White House. In the 1940s, Queen Wilhelmina of the Netherlands saw him when she was visiting President Franklin D. Roosevelt. She was awakened by a knock on her door. When she opened it, there stood the ghost of Abraham Lincoln. She immediately fainted. When she awoke, he was gone.

William Wallace Lincoln

In 1862, Lincoln's son William died in the White House from typhoid fever. He was only 11 years old. His mother, Mary Todd Lincoln, claimed his ghost visited her every night.

"I Will Do It"

ELVEY FARM, PLUCKLEY, ENGLAND

Residents of Pluckley, England, are used to seeing ghosts in the middle of the night. Countless spirit sightings have made it the country's most haunted village. The 75-acre (30-ha) Elvey Farm may be the reason why.

Elvey Farm

It was an otherwise normal day in 1900 at the Elvey Farm. The owner, Edward Brett, calmly told his wife, "I will do it." She wasn't sure what he meant. Edward turned and silently walked to the dairy barn. Later that day, his wife discovered his dead body. Edward had shot himself.

In the years since Edward's death, Elvey Farm was turned into a hotel. To this day, guests claim to hear Edward's chilling last words—"I will do it"—whispered in the dead of night. Many say his ghost still lingers on the property.

Another disturbing spirit also plagues Elvey Farm. Long ago, Robert DuBois was a notorious bandit. He was known for hiding behind trees on the farm before attacking his victims. Finally, Robert was captured and stabbed to death by angry townspeople. They pinned his body to a tree he used to hide behind. His spirit, however, lives on. Today, visitors to the farmhouse have reported hearing footsteps and floorboards creaking throughout the night. Is Robert's ghost looking for another victim?

> Elvey Farm guests often experience paranormal activity, such as ghost sightings and the smell of burning hay.

The Bell Witch

JOHN BELL FARM, ADAMS, TENNESSEE

The haunting of John Bell's farm began around 1817. For more than 200 years, people have visited the farm to decide for themselves whether it's one of America's spookiest places or not.

This cabin was once located on the John Bell Farm.

One day, John Bell saw a creature near his home that had the body of a dog and the head of a rabbit. John shot at it, but the beast disappeared. That evening, he and his family heard a noise outside. It was a loud scraping, like the sound of huge, bony hands clawing at their farmhouse. The family went to bed but was terrorized as they tried to sleep. Blankets were flung off beds, and the Bell children were slapped and pinched. All the while, a strange voice whispered in the halls.

It soon became clear that this was no ordinary spirit. One night, the poltergeist spoke directly to the Bells. It identified itself as Old Kate Batts' witch. Kate was John Bell's former neighbor. The two had argued about land before she died. Kate had placed a curse on the Bell family and even promised to kill John.

One day, John came down with a mysterious illness. The poltergeist took credit for his failing health. When John died in December 1820, the witch claimed she had poisoned him. At his funeral, her ghostly voice echoed through the church.

John Bell on his deathbed

The Bell Witch may have crossed paths with an American president. Andrew Jackson reportedly visited the Bell Farm to experience the haunting for himself.

27

The Problem with Poison

THE MYRTLES PLANTATION
ST. FRANCISVILLE, LOUISIANA

The Myrtles Plantation is considered one of America's most haunted houses. Many of the ghostly tales about the home may be more fiction than fact, but that doesn't stop the stories from being told—and even being believed.

The Myrtles Plantation

Clarke Woodruff ran the Myrtles Plantation in the early 1800s. He was not kind to the people who worked for him. One time, he caught an enslaved woman named Chloe eavesdropping on one of his conversations. He was so angry that he had one of her ears cut off.

According to legend, rather than get upset, Chloe wanted to find a way to show that she still cared about the Woodruff family. So, Chloe baked them a cake containing a small amount of poisonous flowers. Once they ate it, she imagined she would kindly nurse the sick family back to health. The poison, however, was too strong. Mrs. Woodruff and her two daughters died. When people found out what she did, Chloe was hanged.

Since then, people have claimed Chloe's ghost haunts the Myrtles. A past owner even accidentally took a photo of her. In it, Chloe appears in the turban she wore to cover her missing ear.

The haunted mirror at the Myrtles

According to some people, the spirits of Mrs. Woodruff and her daughters are trapped in a large mirror at the Myrtles. Photographs of it show ghostly handprints inside the mirror's glass. Even after the glass was replaced, the ghostly handprints returned.

A Glamorous Ghost

ASHTON VILLA MANSION, GALVESTON, TEXAS

Many people believe that when a person's spirit returns as a ghost, it appears as the person did at the time of his or her death. The spirit is often even wearing the same clothes. That's good news for Bettie Ashton Brown. She was always dressed like a princess so she would look great as a ghost.

Ashton Villa Mansion

Beautiful Bettie Ashton Brown was born into a wealthy family in 1855. She spent her pampered life at Ashton Villa, buying fancy fans and dresses. She had many boyfriends but never married. Some claim Bettie loved the expensive items she collected more than any man.

After Bettie died in 1920, her beloved mansion was turned into a museum. Her ghost is said to still visit often. A museum worker once came across her arguing with a dark-haired ghost at the piano. He overheard the ghost saying to Bettie, "It is foolish for any man to talk to you about marriage. You couldn't really love anyone." The dark-haired man then disappeared, leaving behind a sobbing Bettie.

Visitors to the museum have been surprised to hear the ghostly sound of piano playing. Perhaps it is Bettie, trying to heal a broken heart.

A museum guide once saw Bettie's ghost on the second floor. She was wearing a gorgeous turquoise evening gown and holding a beautiful fan. Bettie is stylish—even in death.

A Ghostly Murder

HINTERKAIFECK FARM, GRÖBERN, GERMANY

Tucked away in the German countryside, Hinterkaifeck Farm was the home of the Gruber family. Then, the unthinkable happened. Who—or what—is responsible for the ghastly crime?

Hinterkaifeck Farm

It was a cold, dark night in March 1922. While the Gruber family slept, an intruder wielding a mattock killed all five members of the family and their housekeeper.

In the days leading up to the murders, strange things had happened at the farm. House keys went missing. Objects appeared out of nowhere. The housekeeper saw unfamiliar footprints in the snow. Was a stranger hiding on the property? Or did the prints belong to a ghost? Six months earlier, the previous maid had left the farm because she believed it was haunted by an evil spirit.

A mattock

As the police searched for more clues, they turned to bizarre measures. The heads of the victims were removed from their bodies and sent to a psychic! The police hoped the psychic would be able to make the heads talk. Needless to say, the heads turned out to be a dead end. To this day, the brutal murders remain a mystery. Perhaps the killer is a ghost after all.

The police interviewed more than 100 suspects but never found the killer. The Gruber massacre is Germany's most famous unsolved crime.

The Coffin in the Cellar

GAINESWOOD PLANTATION
DEMOPOLIS, ALABAMA

The question isn't whether or not Gaineswood Plantation is haunted—it's by whom? What dark and disturbing history could explain the horror at this southern site?

Gaineswood Plantation

A room inside the plantation house

Some say the spirits of people killed in a steamboat fire in 1858 still roam Gaineswood. Nearly half the passengers died in the disaster. Over the years, many claim to have seen the steamboat rise up out of the nearby Tombigbee River. They say the ghost ship burns with a phantom fire and cries echo into the night.

The plantation's cellar is another ghostly hangout. After the wife of owner General Nathan Whitfield died, he hired nanny Evelyn Carter to care for his children. Evelyn played the piano and adored the children. Sadly, she, too, died a short time later.

General Whitfield had a coffin built and planned to ship Evelyn's body to the nanny's hometown in Virginia for burial. However, bad weather delayed these plans. The body lay in the cellar for weeks. The wait clearly upset Evelyn's ghost. The family heard footsteps climb the cellar stairs. The faint sound of a piano could also be heard echoing through the house.

It took nearly 20 years to build Gaineswood Plantation. It was completed just before the Civil War.

The 2:00 a.m. Train

VILLISCA AXE MURDER HOUSE
VILLISCA, IOWA

What is a ghost? Many people believe it is the spirit of a person who has stayed on Earth after death. Ghost hunters are people who try to find these mysterious spirits. They usually aren't scared of the ghostly activity they discover. Yet, who wouldn't be frightened to relive a brutal murder?

Villisca Axe Murder House

The murder of the Moore family made headlines.

In the early morning hours of June 10, 1912, a stranger entered the Moore family home. He snuck quietly from room to room. By the time he left, eight people had been killed with an axe. The police didn't have enough evidence to charge anyone with the crime. The killer was never caught. Yet some believe his spirit still haunts the house.

Ghost hunters who have spent the night at the Moore house often notice a ghostly fog. It moves from room to room, just as the killer did the night of his crime. It is followed by the awful sound of dripping blood.

These spooky events usually happen at 2:00 a.m. This is the time when a train passes through the town of Villisca. Some believe that the murderer used the noise from the speeding locomotive to mask the sound of his bloody acts. Perhaps the creepy sights and sounds in the middle of the night are actually the killer's ghost reliving his murders more than 100 years later.

In 1930, Homer and Bonnie Ritter rented the house in Villisca. Night after night, Bonnie woke to the strange sight of a man with an axe at the foot of her bed. Homer then began hearing the sound of someone walking up and down the stairs in the middle of the night. The Ritters moved out shortly thereafter.

The White Witch

ROSE HALL GREAT HOUSE
MONTEGO BAY, JAMAICA

In the early 1800s, Annie Palmer married the owner of Rose Hall—a beautiful mansion. The young woman was lucky to live in such a gorgeous home. Unfortunately, those who lived with Annie were not. They would soon know why this cruel woman was called the White Witch of Rose Hall.

Rose Hall Great House

Although she was a small woman, Annie Palmer was powerful. She is thought to have murdered all three of her husbands. She had the enslaved workers on her sugar plantation beaten and tortured for her amusement. Annie even built a dungeon 16 feet (5 m) deep in the middle of her house. She imprisoned workers there who tried to run away. Many of them ended up dying there, too.

In 1831, Annie became interested in a handsome young man. Unfortunately, he liked her housekeeper, Millicent. So, Annie cast a spell on her. Millicent died nine days later. The housekeeper's grandfather was so angry that he strangled Annie to death.

Annie's body was buried in a cement coffin. Yet her spirit remains at Rose Hall. When a family tried to live there in 1905, Annie's ghost supposedly pushed a maid off the balcony to her death. The family fled, and the beautiful home remained empty until 1965, when it was turned into a museum.

The coffin of the White Witch

Even though Rose Hall is now a museum, the White Witch is still scaring people more than 175 years after her death. Annie's ghost is said to slam doors and windows, turn water on and off, and even appear to some visitors.

A Bloody Battle

DUPREY FARMHOUSE
NORTH WOODSTOCK, CONNECTICUT

When Charles and Florence Viner bought the Duprey Farmhouse in 1951, the place was in ruins. The home's spooky setting proved perfect for a ghostly battle. As the Viners would soon learn, some fights never end—not even after death!

The Duprey Farmhouse is also known as the Brickyard Farmhouse because it's located on Brickyard Road.

One afternoon, Florence Viner and her 11-year-old daughter, Sandra, were alone in the house. To their surprise, they heard what sounded like footsteps upstairs. "It must be the house settling," Mrs. Viner said, trying to calm Sandra's nerves. Suddenly, they heard two loud thuds overhead. As time went by, the strange noises continued. Guests who stayed at the house also heard footsteps and thuds.

Another day, Florence removed old wallpaper from an upstairs guest room. Underneath the paper, she discovered a red stain. Paint, she thought, and tried to scrub it away. Then, she looked closer. It was not red paint at all. It was blood!

Florence later discovered that the farmhouse was originally the Lyons Tavern and dated back to the 1700s. She also learned a shocking secret. Two men had once fought in an upstairs room and both died in the bloody swordfight. The upstairs noises now made sense—the two loud thuds were the bodies of the men as each dropped dead to the floor!

After spending just one night in the farmhouse, Florence's mother declared, "I'll never sleep in this house again. Why, it's haunted! Someone kept walking through my bedroom."

A World of . . .

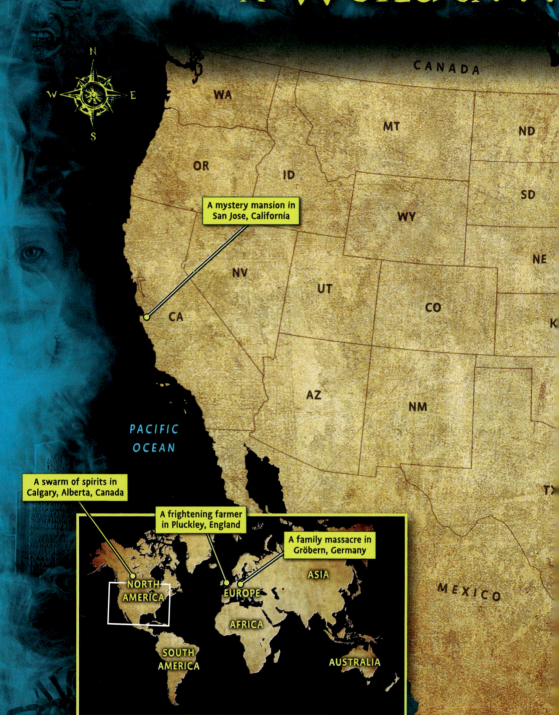

- A mystery mansion in San Jose, California
- A swarm of spirits in Calgary, Alberta, Canada
- A frightening farmer in Pluckley, England
- A family massacre in Gröbern, Germany

Hauntings at Home

43

Glossary

anthropologist a person who studies the different characteristics and beliefs of people around the world

apparition a ghost or ghostlike image

artifacts objects of historical interest made by people

assassin a person who kills a politically important person

burial ground land where dead bodies are buried

Civil War the war in the United States between the southern states and the northern states, which lasted from 1861 to 1865

corpse a dead body

cursed bringing unhappiness or bad luck

descendent a person who is related to someone who lived in the past

dungeon a dark prison cell, usually underground

eavesdropping secretly listening to another person's conversation

evidence objects or information that can be used to prove whether something is true

fiction a story that has characters and events that are made up

ghastly horrible and shocking

gloom a sense of sadness

inn a small hotel

legend a story handed down from long ago that is often based on some facts but cannot be proven true

lore a collection of traditional stories about a topic

mansion a large and grand house

massacre a brutal killing of many people

mattock a tool for digging that is shaped like a pickaxe

medium a person through whom others seek to communicate with the spirits of the dead

notorious known by many for doing bad things

overseers people who were in charge of enslaved workers

pampered treated with too much care and attention

paranormal events that are not able to be scientifically explained

plagues causes harm

plantation a large farm where crops, such as cotton, coffee, or tea, are grown

poltergeist a disruptive ghost that makes itself known in a home by making loud noises and moving objects

psychic a person sensitive to nonphysical forces and who can communicate with the spirits of the dead

resident a person who lives in a certain place

revenge punishment for something that has been unfairly done

ruins what is left of something that has collapsed or been destroyed

sacred holy

spectral ghostly

spell words that are supposed to have magical powers

spirit a supernatural creature, such as a ghost

tavern a place where liquor is sold

turban a covering for one's head, often made by wrapping a long scarf or piece of cloth around the head

turquoise a blue-green color

yellow fever a deadly disease caused by a virus that is spread through the bite of a mosquito

Read More

Morrison, Marie. *The White House Is Haunted! (Haunted History)*. New York: PowerKids Press, 2020.

Snowden, Matilda. *Investigating Ghosts in Houses (Investigating Ghosts)*. Hallandale, FL: Mitchell Lane Publishers, 2021.

Wilkins, Ebony Joy. *Perron Family Haunting: The Ghost Story That Inspired Horror Movies (Real-Life Ghost Stories)*. North Mankato, MN: Capstone Press, 2020.

Wood, Alix. *Ghostly Mansions (World's Scariest Places)*. New York: Gareth Stevens Publishing, 2020.

Learn More Online

1. Go to **www.factsurfer.com** or scan the QR code below.

2. Enter "**Hauntings at Home**" into the search box.

3. Click on the cover of this book to see a list of websites.

Index

Amityville House 18-19
Ashton Villa Mansion 30-31
Batts, Kate 27
Bell, John 26-27
Bell Witch 26-27, 43
Booth, John Wilkes 23
Borden, Abby 12-13
Borden, Andrew 12-13
Borden, Lizzie 13
Brown, Bettie Ashton 30-31
Chretien Point Plantation 6-7
Civil War 7, 21, 35
Deane House, The 16-17
DeFeo, Ronald, Jr. 19
Duprey Farmhouse 40
Elvey Farm 24-25
Gaineswood Plantation 34-35
Hinterkaifeck Farm 32
Jackson, Andrew 22, 27
Jesse Merwin Farmhouse 10
John Bell Farm 26-27
Legend of Sleepy Hollow, The 11
Lincoln, Abraham 22-23
Lincoln, Mary Todd 22-23
Lizzie Borden House 12-13
Lutz family 19
Magnolia Plantation 20-21
Merwin, Jesse 11
Myrtles Plantation, The 28-29
Old Arnold Estate 14-15
Palmer, Annie 38-39
poltergeist 18, 27
Rose Hall Great House 38-39
Sherman, Bathsheba 15
Villisca Axe Murder House 36
White House, The 22-23
Winchester House 8-9
Winchester, Sarah 8-9
Winchester, William 9
Woodruff, Clarke 29

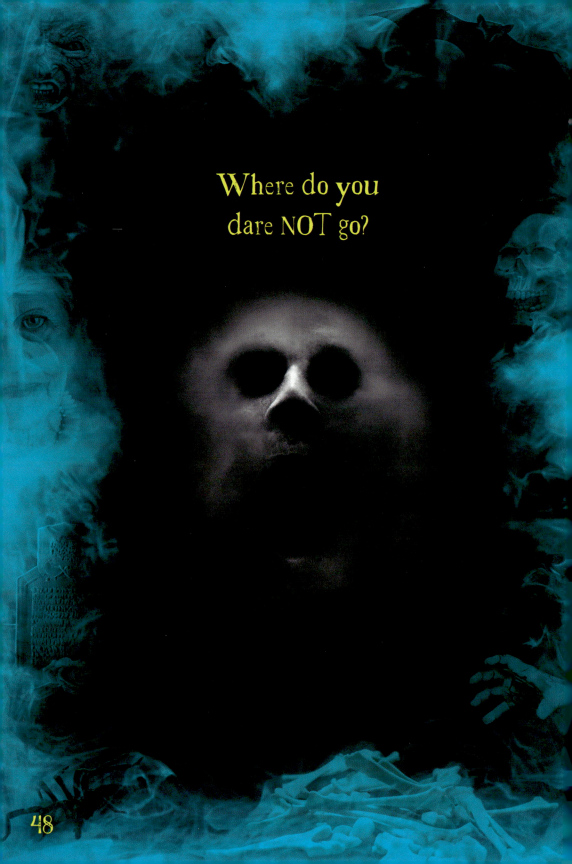